MUM'S T

We Knew You Had It In You

MUM'S THE WORD

or

We Knew You Had It In You

Observations on Motherhood

• JASMINE BIRTLES •

Michael O'Mara Books Limited
In association with SHE MAGAZINE

First published in 1995 by
Michael O'Mara Books Limited
9 Lion Yard
Tremadoc Road
London SW4 7NQ

ISBN 1-85479-763-8

A CIP catalogue record for this book is available from the
British Library

1 3 5 7 9 10 8 6 4 2

Typeset and Designed by
Keystroke, Jacaranda Lodge, Wolverhampton
Printed and bound in England by Cox & Wyman, Reading

Contents

Familiarity
breeds children

Parenthood is a lot easier to get in to than out of.

• BRUCE LANSKY •

Vasectomies and condoms are as safe for women as anything based on men's behaviour can be.

• SPARE RIB MAGAZINE •

A crying baby is the best form of birth control.

• CAROLE TABBRON •

From the number of children in evidence it appears that people have them at the drop of a hat – for surely were they to give this matter its due attention they would act with greater decorum.

• FRAN LEBOWITZ •

*A*nyone believing in the
Virgin Birth is
labouring under a misconception.

• ANONYMOUS •

*T*he command 'Be fruitful and
multiply' was promulgated
according to our authorities, when the
population of the world consisted of
two people.

• DEAN INGE, BRITISH CHURCHMAN •

*F*amily Planning – Please Use
Rear Entrance.

● SIGN OUTSIDE A HEALTH CENTRE ●

*C*hildren in the front seat cause
accidents. Accidents in the
back seat cause children.

● ANONYMOUS ●

*I*t is now quite lawful for a
Catholic woman to
avoid pregnancy by a resort to
mathematics, though she is still
forbidden to resort to physics and
chemistry.

• H L MENCKEN •

Him
'How do you like your
eggs in the morning?'

Her
'Unfertilized.'

• ANONYMOUS •

Contraceptives should be used on every conceivable occasion.

• SPIKE MILLIGAN •

Protestant women may take the Pill. Roman Catholic women must keep taking the Tablet.

• IRENE THOMAS •

*W*hat do you call people who use the rhythm method? Parents.

• ANONYMOUS •

*B*irth control that really works. Every night before we go to bed we spend an hour with our kids.

• ROSEANNE ARNOLD •

I want to tell you a terrific story about oral contraception.
I asked this girl to sleep with me and she said, 'No.'

• WOODY ALLEN •

I can't mate in captivity.

• GLORIA STEINEM •

Bump!

*L*ife is tough enough
without having
someone kick
you from the inside.

• RITA RUDNER •

I think she decided to go into show business when she was an embryo, she kicked so much.

• JUDY GARLAND ON LIZA MINNELLI •

*I*n Australia, breeding is something
we do with dogs.

• KATHY LETTE •

*T*hink of stretch marks as
pregnancy service
stripes.

• JOYCE ARMOR •

The birthing experience

It's an experience every man should have. We don't know what a woman goes through. We just sit back after it's all over and pass out cigars and say, 'See what I did.'

• BEN VEREEN •

What's the difference between a man and childbirth?

One is an excruciating, painful, unbearable experience; the other is just having a baby.

• ANONYMOUS •

*C*hildbirth is an occupational
hazard of being a wife.

• PRINCESS ANNE •

*I*f pregnancy were a book they
would cut the last two
chapters.

• NORA EPHRON •

*D*eath and taxes and childbirth!
There's never any
convenient time for any of them!

• MARGARET MITCHELL •

*I*n my last stage of labour I threatened to take my husband to court for concealing a lethal weapon in his boxer shorts.

• LINDA FITERMAN •

I'd be happy to stand next to any man I know in one of those labour rooms the size of a Volkswagen trunk and whisper, 'No, dear, you don't really need the Demerol; just relax and do your second-stage breathing.'

• ANNA QUINDLEN •

Having a baby is like taking your bottom lip and pulling it over your head.

• CAROL BURNETT •

Serves me right for putting all my eggs in one bastard.

• DOROTHY PARKER •
ON HER WAY TO HAVE AN ABORTION

I was Caesarean-born. You can't really tell, although whenever I leave a house I go out through a window.

• STEVEN WRIGHT •

We ourselves have only one child, because after Beth experienced the Joy and Wonder of natural childbirth, she decided not to experience it again until modern science invents a method whereby the man has the contractions.

• DAVE BARRY •

If men had to have babies, they would only ever have one.

• PRINCESS OF WALES •

Let's face it, if God had meant men to have children, he would have given them PVC aprons.

• VICTORIA WOOD •

Somewhere on this globe, every ten seconds, there is a woman giving birth to a child. She must be found and stopped.

• SAM LEVENSON •

Congrats! We all knew you had it in you.

• DOROTHY PARKER •

To enter life by way of the vagina is as good a way as any.

• HENRY MILLER •

If you have more than four children
you're overbearing.

• ANONYMOUS •

To my embarrassment, I was born
in bed with a lady.

• WILSON MIZNER •

I had a Jewish delivery: they
knock you out with the
first pain; they wake you up when
the hairdresser shows.

• JOAN RIVERS •

Natural Birth: A case of stiff upper labia.

• KATHY LETTE •

Childbirth classes neglect to teach one critical skill: How to breathe, count, and swear at the same time.

• LINDA FITERMAN •

*W*hat do they think my uterus is
   – a tracking device?

• ROSEANNE ARNOLD •

*I*t is somehow reassuring to
   discover that the word
'travel' is derived from 'travail',
denoting the pains of childbirth.

• JESSICA MITFORD •

*W*hen I had almost reached
my term, I looked like
a rat dragging a stolen egg.

• COLETTE •

*M*y obstetrician was so dumb
that when I gave
birth he forgot to cut the cord.
For a year that kid followed
me everywhere. It was like
having a dog on a leash.

• JOAN RIVERS •

A baby is born

*W*hen I was born I was so
   surprised I didn't
talk for a year and a half.

• GRACIE ALLEN •

*W*omen have babies because
   they can't think of
anything better to do.

• LORD BEAUMONT OF WHITLEY •

It sometimes happens, even in the best of families, that a baby is born. This is not necessarily cause for a alarm. The important thing its to keep your wits about you and borrow some money.

• ELINOR GOULDING SMITH •

I think of birth as the search for a larger apartment.

• RITA MAE BROWN •

*B*abies leak. From both ends.

• BRUCE LANSKY •

A soiled baby with a neglected nose cannot be conscientiously regarded as a thing of beauty.

• MARK TWAIN •

A baby's like a new car. It has two-lung power, free squealing, scream-lined body, changeable seat covers and an easily flooded carburettor.

• BOB MONKHOUSE •

*M*en who have fought in the
world's bloodiest
wars . . . are apt to faint at
the sight of a foul diaper.

• GARY D CHRISTENSON •

*P*eople who say they sleep
like babies usually
don't have one.

• MOYRA BREMNER •

*B*abies: A loud noise at one
end and no sense of
responsibility at the other.

• FATHER RONALD KNOX •

The only time a woman really succeeds in changing a man is when he's a baby.

• NATALIE WOOD •

I learned to walk as a baby, and I haven't had a lesson since.

• MARILYN MONROE •

Training babies is mostly a matter of pot-luck.

• BOB MONKHOUSE •

Tom, Dick
or Harry?

My wife wanted to call our
daughter Sue,
but I felt that in our family
that was usually a verb.

• DENNIS WOLFBERG •

*Now why did you name your baby John?
Every Tom, Dick or
Harry is named John.*

• SAMUEL GOLDWYN •

After giving birth to quadruplets the tired mother named them Adolph, Rudolph, Getoff and Stayoff.

• ANONYMOUS •

God *could not be*
everywhere –
that's why he made
mothers

*A mother! What are we worth
really? They all grow
up whether you look after
them or not.*

• CHRISTINA STEAD •

*Being a mother is a profession
just like being a doctor
or a lawyer except that if you
have several children it's more like
being an Indian chief.*

• ANONYMOUS •

I'm at that stage of motherhood
where I'm putting the kids
under the sink and the lethal house-
hold substances within reach.

• KATHY LETTE •

*P*eople said I'd slim down
quickly. Nobody told
me it was because I'd never
have time to eat.

• ANONYMOUS •

*The only thing that seems eternal
and natural in motherhood
is ambivalence.*

• JANE LAZARRE •

*A mother is neither cocky, nor
proud, because
she knows the school principal may
call at any minute to report that her
child has just driven a motorcycle
through the gymnasium.*

• MARY KAY BLAKELY •

If evolution really works, how come
mothers only have two hands?

• MILTON BERLE •

It's not easy being a mother.
If it were easy, fathers
would do it.

• DOROTHY ON THE GOLDEN GIRLS •

There is no such thing as a non-working mother.

• HESTER MUNDIS •

Because I am a mother, I am capable of being shocked; as I never was when I was not one.

• MARGARET ATWOOD •

Hey, the way I figure it is this: if the kids are still alive by the time my husband comes home, I've done my job.

• ROSEANNE ARNOLD •

Sometimes when I look at my children I say to myself, 'Lillian, you should have stayed a virgin.'

• LILLIAN CARTER (MOTHER OF JIMMY) •

*A*ny mother could perform the jobs of several air-traffic controllers with ease.

• LISA ALTHER •

*W*hoever thinks a housewife has no superiors to answer to has never raised children.

• ANONYMOUS •

There's only one pretty child in the world, and every mother has it.

• PROVERB •

All mothers share the magical ability to divine when a child is faking a tummyache.

• NORMA PETERSON •

*Mothers are fonder than fathers
of their children
because they are more certain
they are their own.*

• ARISTOTLE •

*. . . everybody's momma done better
than anybody had any right to expect
she would. And that's the truth!*

• JUNE JORDAN •

*S*etting a good
example

*S*ons branch out, but one woman
leads to another.

• MARGARET ATWOOD •

*M*y husband knows so much
about rearing children
that I've suggested he has the next one
and I'll sit back and give advice.

• PRINCESS OF WALES •

I don't approve of smacking –
I just use a cattle-prod.

• JENNY ECLAIR •

It seems a shame that most parents
weren't given their neighbours'
children, because those are the only
ones they know how to raise.

• BOB MONKHOUSE •

How do you get your children
to do what you say?
Say nothing.

• ANONYMOUS •

If your children are giving
you a headache, follow
the directions on the aspirin bottle,
especially the part that says: Keep
away from children.

• RODNEY DANGERFIELD •

Never play peek-a-boo with a child on a long plane trip. There's no end to the game. Finally I grabbed him by the bib and said, 'Look. It's always gonna be me.'

• RITA RUDNER •

Reasoning with a two-year-old is about as productive as changing seats on the Titanic.

• ROBERT SCOTELLARO •

There are hundreds of different toilet-training methods – probably because none of them work.

• BRUCE LANSKY •

An effective guilt tactic is suddenly to yell, 'I see you!' when your children are in a different room.

• BILL DODDS •

*H*ow are children like waiters?
They never come when
you call them.

• ANONYMOUS •

I want to have children while my
parents are still young
enough to take care of them.

• RITA RUDNER •

If you want your children to listen, try talking softly –
to someone else.

• ANN LANDERS •

*C*leaning your house while the kids are still growing is
like shovelling the walk before it stops snowing.

• PHYLLIS DILLER •

*Before I got married I had six
theories about bringing
up children; now I have
six children and no theories.*

• JOHN WILMOT, ENGLISH POET •

*The moment you have children
yourself, you forgive
your parents everything.*

• SUSAN HILL, NOVELIST •

I didn't make the same mistakes
my parents made when
they raised me. I was too
busy making new ones.

• BRUCE LANSKY •

T here's a time when you have
to explain to your children
why they're born, and it's a
marvellous thing if you know the
reason by then.

• HAZEL SCOTT •

*D*efinition of childish behaviour –
anyone doing what we only
wish we could still do.

• ANONYMOUS •

*M*y sister's pretty stupid. She
keeps having a baby
each year because she says she
doesn't want the youngest one
to get spoiled.

• ANONYMOUS •

*W*hen I meet a man I ask
myself, 'Is this the
man I want my children to
spend their weekends with?'

● RITA RUDNER ●

*I*s a Pas de Deux the father of twins?

● ANONYMOUS ●

It goes without saying that you should never have more children than you have car windows.

• ERMA BOMBECK •

I never got along with my dad. Kids used to come up to me and say, 'My dad can beat up your dad.' I'd say, 'Yeah? When?'

• BILL HICKS •

*W*e modern, sensitive husbands
realize that it's very unfair
to place the entire child-care burden
on our wives, so many of us are
starting to assume maybe three per
cent of it.

• DAVE BARRY •

I haven't changed that many
diapers. A few, just a few.
I don't consider that my job.

• NICK NOLTE •

*P*arents are not interested
in justice, they are
interested in quiet.

• BILL COSBY •

*C*hildren are natural copiers – they
behave just like their
parents, however much we try to
teach them not to.

• JEAN BIRTLES (TOP NOTCH NANNIES AND
BRILLIANT BABYSITTERS) •

I have found the best way to give advice to your children is to find out what they want and then advise them to do it.

• HARRY S TRUMAN •

*B*efore I had kids I went home after work to rest.
Now I go to work to rest.

• SIMON RUDDELL •

*D*ear God, I pray for patience.
And I want it right now.

• ORBEN ARNOLD •

*N*ever raise your hand to your children; it leaves your mid-section unprotected.

• ROBERT ORBEN •

I have an intense desire to return to the womb. Anybody's.

• WOODY ALLEN •

*N*o matter how old a mother is she watches her middle-aged children for signs of improvement.

• FLORIDA SCOTT-MAXWELL •

*I*f you had never been hated by
your child, you have never
been a parent.

● BETTE DAVIS ●

*O*ne of the things I've discovered
in general about raising kids
is that they really don't give a damn
if you walked five miles to school.
They want to deal with what's
happening now.

● PATTY DUKE ●

A successful parent is one who raises a child who grows up and is able to pay for her or his own psychoanalysis.

• NORA EPHRON •

T here are three ways to get something done: do it yourself, hire someone, or forbid your kids to do it.

• MONTA CRANE •

Literature is mostly about having sex and not much about having children; life is the other way round.

• DAVID LODGE •

Setting a good example for children takes all the fun out of middle age.

• WILLIAM FEATHER •

The quickest way for a parent to get a child's attention is to sit down and look comfortable.

• LANE LOINGHOUSE •

Disguising a vegetable as a French fry

*T*oddlers are more likely to eat
healthy food if they find
it on the floor.

• JAN BLAUSTONE •

*I*n general, my children refused
to eat anything that hadn't
danced on TV.

• ERMA BOMBECK •

*As a child, my family's menu
consisted of two
choices: take it or leave it.*

• BUDDY HACKETT •

*Ask your child what he
wants for dinner
only if he is buying.*

• FRAN LEBOWITZ •

*T*he secret to feeding you child is
learning how to disguise
a vegetable as a French fry.

• JAN BLAUSTONE •

*T*he best way to prevent your
children from eating fatty,
greasy, disgusting, unhealthy
food is: Don't let them eat from
your plate.

• BILL DODDS •

I always wondered why babies
spend so much time sucking
their thumbs. Then I tasted baby food.

• ROBERT ORBEN •

*T*he Broody
Bunch

*My kids never had the advantage
I had. I was born poor.*

• KIRK DOUGLAS •

*My family weren't the Brady
Bunch. They were the
Broody Bunch.*

• SANDRA BERNHADT •

Before we can leave our parents,
they stuff our heads like
the suitcases which they jam-pack
with homemade underwear.

• MAXINE HONG KINGSTON •

I always wanted to do what my mother did – get dressed up, shoot people, fall in the mud. I never considered anything else.

● CARRIE FISHER ●

It was no great tragedy being Judy Garland's daughter. I had tremendously interesting childhood years – except they had little to do with being a child.

● LIZA MINNELLI ●

At last I've seen a toy that was labelled accurately. It said, 'Recommended for children aged 3–6 provided they can get their hands on £48.50.

. . . a small child can go for weeks without going to the bathroom at home, but once you hit the road, it becomes pretty much a full-time occupation.

• DAVE BARRY •

My mother loved children – she
would have given
anything if I had been one.

● GROUCHO MARX ●

The way that some children of
prominent celebrities write
books critical of their parents helps
you understand why certain species in
this world eat their young.

● RONALD REAGAN ●

*C*hildren only want high
technology toys
nowadays. My son has an
imaginary playmate that
requires batteries.

• ANONYMOUS •

*A*n ugly baby is a very nasty
object, and the
prettiest is frightful when
undressed.

• QUEEN VICTORIA •

*I*f you want to bring your family close, buy a smaller car

*Never lend your car to anyone
to whom you have
given birth.*

• ERMA BOMBECK •

*I bought my child a toy that was
absolutely guaranteed to
be unbreakable. He used it to break
all his other toys.*

• ANONYMOUS •

As my children got older, I got used to buying Christmas presents that a) I couldn't spell, b) had no idea what they were used for, and c) leaked grease.

• ERMA BOMBECK •

. . . my eight-year-old bought a bicycle with the money he saved by not smoking.

• PHYLLIS DILLER •

*W*hy is it that the more
expensive a toy is,
the more inclined a child is
to play with the box it came in?

• ANONYMOUS •

I was doing the family grocery
shopping accompanied by
two children, an event I hope to see
included in the Olympics in the
near future.

• ANNA QUINDLEN •

A child is someone who stands
halfway between an
adult an a TV set.

• ANONYMOUS •

*N*o matter what the critics say,
it's hard to believe
that a television programme
which keeps four children
quiet for an hour can be all bad.

• BERYL PFIZER •

*Some new toys are so
complicated that
only a child can operate them.*

• ANONYMOUS •

*We've been having some trouble
with the school bus.
It keeps bringing the kids back.*

• BRUCE LANSKY •

*C*hildren are rarely in the
position to lend one
a truly interesting sum of money.
There are, however, exceptions,
and such children are an excellent
addition to any party.

• FRAN LEBOWITZ •

*G*ames to play with the kids in the car: 'Churchmouse' – first one who makes the slightest peep loses; 'Telepathy' – everybody tries to send their thoughts to everybody else without speaking; 'Foxhole' – children pretend that they are in a foxhole on a battlefield and therefore must not utter a sound.

• ROZ CHAST •

A babysitter is a teenage girl you hire to let your children do whatever they want.

• HENNY YOUNGMAN •

I've found out what I don't like about family holidays – family.

• ANONYMOUS •

*W*hen my kids become wild
and unruly, I use a nice,
safe playpen. When they're
finished, I climb out.

• ERMA BOMBECK •

*I*nsanity is hereditary – you get it
from your kids.

• ANONYMOUS •

*B*irthday parties are a lot like childbirth. After both events you solemnly swear you'll never make that mistake again.

• LINDA FITERMAN •

I threw a birthday party for
my little boy with
twenty children and ten adults.
After half and hour there
was mess on the floor, on
the walls and on the ceiling
– then the children started.

• DOLLY DUPREE •

I take my children everywhere;
but they always find their
way back home.

• ROBERT ORBEN •

C hildren make the most desirable
opponents in Scrabble as
they are both easy to beat and
fun to cheat.

• FRAN LEBOWITZ •

You know you've lost control
when you're the one who
goes to your room.

• BABS BELL HAJDUSIEWICZ •

There are two classes of travel
– first class, and with
children.

• ROBERT BENCHLEY •

Children are unpredictable

*A*n advantage of having one
child is you always
know who did it.

• BABS HELL HAJDUSIEWICZ •

*E*ven when freshly washed and
relieved of all obvious
confections, children tend to be
sticky. One can only assume that
this has something to do with not
smoking enough.

• FRAN LEBOWITZ •

There are only two things a child will share willingly – communicable diseases and his mother's age.

• DR BENJAMIN SPOCK •

What is a home without children? Quiet.

• HENNY YOUNGMAN •

*I*f you wonder where you child left
his rollerskates, try walking
around the house in the dark.

• LEOPOLD FECHTNER •

*C*hildren are usually small in
stature which makes
them quite useful for getting at
those hard-to-reach places.

• FRAN LEBOWITZ •

*C*hildren – they never put off
till tomorrow what will
keep them from going
to bed tonight.

• BOB MONKHOUSE •

*W*hen I was a kid my parents
moved a lot – but
I always found them.

• RODNEY DANGERFIELD •

*T*here's one thing about children –
they never go around
showing snapshots of their
grandparents.

• LEOPOLD FECHTNER •

*C*hildren are a great comfort in
your old age – and they
help you reach it faster too.

• LIONEL KAUFFMAN •

*A*dorable children are considered
to be the general property
of the human race. (Rude children
belong to their mothers.)

• JUDITH MARTIN •

I love children, especially when
they cry, for then someone
takes them away.

• NANCY MITFORD •

*M*y kids would never share
anything of their
own free will – except germs.

• BRUCE LANSKY •

*D*on't tell your two-year-old
she's driving you nuts.
She just might say, 'Mama nuts',
to everyone she meets.

• JAN BLAUSTONE •

It is still quite possible to stand in a throng of children without once detecting even the faintest whiff of an exciting, rugged after-shave or cologne.

● FRAN LEBOWITZ ●

Nothing brings out a toddler's devotion to a toy she has abandoned more quickly than another child playing with it.

● ROBERT SCOTELLARO ●

*C*hildren aren't happy with nothing to ignore. And that's what parents were created for.

• OGDEN NASH •

*C*hildren are unpredictable. You never know what inconsistency they're going to catch you in next.

• FRANKLIN P JONES •

*A*dults are always asking children what they want to be when they grow up – they're looking for ideas.

• PAUL POUNDSTONE •

*A*ny kid will run any errand for you if you ask at bedtime.

• RED SKELTON •

I've got two wonderful children –
and two out of five isn't too
bad.

• HENNY YOUNGMAN •

I have seen my kid struggle into the
kitchen in the morning with
outfits that need only one
accessory . . . an empty gin bottle.

• ERMA BOMBECK •

Missing a generation

*I*f your baby is 'beautiful and
perfect, never cries or
fusses, sleeps on schedule and burps
on demand, and is an angel all the
time', you're the grandma.

• THERESA BLOOMINGDALE •

A grandmother will put a sweater
on you when she is cold,
feed you when she is hungry, and put
you to bed when she is tired.

• ERMA BOMBECK •

Grandma know best, but no one ever listens.

• MARY MCBRIDE •

Why did the old man have a vasectomy?

He didn't want any more grandchildren.

• ANONYMOUS •

*T*he reason grandparents and grandchildren get along so well is that they have a common enemy. The mother.

• SAM LEVENSON •

*Y*our sons weren't made to like you. That's what grandchildren are for.

• JANE SMILEY •

*W*hen I was
a kid . . .

I knew I was an unwanted baby
    when I saw that my bath
toys were a toaster and a radio.

• JOAN RIVERS •

*M*y parents put a live teddy bear
    in my crib.

• WOODY ALLEN •

We *had a quicksand box*
in our backyard.
I was an only child, eventually.

• STEVEN WRIGHT •

I *was so ugly as a kid, I had to trick-*
or-treat over the phone.

• RODNEY DANGERFIELD •

*W*hen I was a kid, we were
evicted so often we had
to buy curtains that matched
the sidewalks.

• MILTON BERLE •

*I*n kindergarten I flunked
sandpile.

• JOEY BISHOP •

I'll never forget my youth.
I was the teacher's pet.
She couldn't afford a dog.

• RODNEY DANGERFIELD •

*W*hen I was young I had the
cutest little button nose,
but they couldn't feed me.
It was buttoned to my lower lip.

• HENNY YOUNGMAN •

*W*hen I was a kid, I was so poor
I had to wear my brother's
hand-me-downs – at the same
time he was wearing them.

• REDD FOXX •

I came from a very poor family.
They couldn't afford to have
children; so our neighbour had me.

• HENNY YOUNGMAN •

*W*hen I was young, if any of
us kids got sick, my
mother would bring out the
chicken soup. Of course, that
didn't work for broken
bones. For broken bones she
gave boiled beef.

• GEORGE BURNS •

Anonymous childhood experiences

I didn't like to play hide-and-seek
when I was young.
My invisible playmate always won.

I never liked hide-and-seek.
*Not since the time I hid in
the cupboard and my family
moved.*

My best game as a child was
tiddlywinks until
*I had a career-ending injury . . .
I sprained my wink finger.
It could have been worse,
I could have broken my tiddly.*

*M*y parents were clever. They used to buy us batteries for Christmas and put a sign on them that said, 'Toys not included'.

*M*y mother put so much starch in everything. I remember one night my brother fell out of bed and broke his pajamas.

My mother once said, 'Tell the truth and shame the devil'. I once told the truth and shamed my father.

When I played football, I was known as 'Crazy Legs' until I was twelve years old. That's when I learned to put my shorts on with the zip at the front.

I was very poor as a child.
My parents were
wealthy but I was poor.

*W*hen I was a child we were so
poor all we had to wear
were hand-me-downs which
was tough on me since
I was an only child.

I never experienced poverty
as a child – my parents
couldn't afford it.

I gave my children everything
I never had as a child
– and they laughed at them.

As a child I was so rich my parents bought me a chauffeur-driven bicycle.

My mummy used to use kisses to make the hurts go away. My doctor says he'll stick with aspirin.

Please contact our Sales Department for a
FREE catalogue, containing information on
other titles published by

MICHAEL O'MARA BOOKS LIMITED
9 Lion Yard
Tremadoc Road
London SW4 7NQ

Tel: **0171-720-8643**
Fax: **0171-627-8953**